HAPPY HANDS AND FEET

Art Projects For Young Children

by
Cindy Mitchell

Incentive Publications, Inc.
Nashville, TN

Illustrated by Susan Eaddy
Cover by Susan Eaddy
Edited by Sally Sharpe

Library of Congress Catalog Card Number 88-82903
ISBN 0-86530-062-3

TABLE OF CONTENTS

PREFACE

All of the projects in this book are for hands and feet only! These exciting multi-sensory activities will stimulate sensory awareness as well as foster individual creative abilities. Even the least artistically oriented child will enjoy the thrill of feeling and experimenting with wet, squishy paint. Children will explore the world of color, design, and texture as they develop a sense of self by creating unique paintings that only they can create!

This book contains projects for every season, many holidays, and fun "critters" as well as ideas for expanding many of the projects. All of the activities require little more than tempera paint, paintbrushes, and construction paper. What's more, step-by-step instructions and finished-product illustrations help simplify preparation and presentation time. The "helpful hints" on the following page will alert you to the simplest procedures and techniques. Included are tips for sensible set up, no-mess precautions, and quick and easy cleanup.

These hands and feet painting creations make impressive classroom or hall displays as well as treasured gifts to send home. Best of all, you'll discover that painting can be a wonderful way to nuture a child's creative ability and self-esteem!

HELPFUL HINTS

- Cover the work area, including the floor, with newspaper.
- Use aluminum pie tins or Styrofoam trays for paint trays.
- Use Styrofoam egg cartons as paint trays when using more than one color of paint.
- Keep a pan of soapy water and paper towels nearby for quick wash-ups.
- Keep wet cloths or paper towels handy to quickly wipe up spills and messes.
- Provide the children with paint smocks to protect their clothing. Use old shirts or plastic bags with holes cut for heads and arms.

- Add a small amount of liquid soap or detergent to the paint for easy cleanup.
- Discourage the children from dipping their hands in paint unless specifically instructed to do so. Painting hands or feet with paintbrushes gives more color control and prevents the use of excessive paint, which can spoil a print.

- Use a different paintbrush for each color to prevent color mixing.

- Experiment with different kinds of paper. Paper plates work well and also "frame" the prints.
- Instruct the children to press their hands and feet firmly on the paper when making prints to ensure clarity.
- Remind the children to keep their hands and feet still while printing and to lift their hands and feet straight up to prevent smudging.
- Encourage the children to experiment with various color combinations.
- Allow older or more mature children to paint their own hands or feet and those of classmates. Other children will require more teacher involvement.
- Allow the children to make choices and to think independently.

AN APPLE FOR THE TEACHER

MATERIALS:
- red and green tempera paint
- Manila paper (8½" x 11")
- ½" - 1" flat paintbrushes (one for each color)
- small, flat container
- newspaper

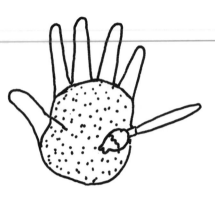

DIRECTIONS:
1. Spread newspaper over the work area.
2. Paint palm with red paint.
3. Press palm in the center of the paper to make a print.
4. Pour a small amount of green paint into a flat container.
5. Dip pad of thumb in green paint and press above the apple print to make a leaf and stem.

USE:
- The apple prints may be used to encourage attendance, good work habits, or some other behavior. Cut out the apples, write the students' names on them, and display them on a large construction paper tree attached to the wall. As long as a child maintains the behavior, his or her apple remains on the tree.

FALL FOLIAGE

MATERIALS:

- tempera paint (brown, gold, orange, yellow, red, etc.)
- Manila paper, construction paper, or newsprint (8½" x 11")
- ½" - 1" flat paintbrushes (one for each color)
- aluminum pie tins or Styrofoam trays
- newspaper

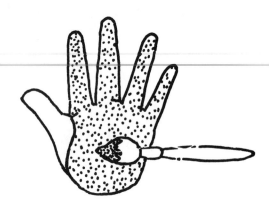

DIRECTIONS:

1. Spread newspaper over the work area.
2. Pour small amounts of assorted autumn colors of tempera paint into paint trays.
3. Paint palm and inside of fingers of one hand, excluding thumb, with brown paint.
4. Press hand on the paper so that the palm forms a trunk and the fingers form branches.
5. Dip pad of thumb in paint, one color at a time, and "stamp" leaves on the branches.

USE:

- Let the children create their own autumn landscape on a wall in the classroom. Attach a green construction paper hillside to the wall. Have the children cut out their trees and tape them to the hillside.

GOOFY GHOST

MATERIALS:

- black and white tempera paint
- black construction paper (8½" x 11")
- pan of soapy water
- ½" - 1" flat paintbrushes (one for each color)
- newspaper

DIRECTIONS:

1. Spread a thick layer of newspaper over the work area.
2. Place a pan of soapy water near the work area.
3. Paint the bottom of a bare foot, including toes, with white paint.
4. Press painted foot in the center of a sheet of black construction paper.
5. Dip index finger in black paint and press on the heel of the ghost print to make two eyes.

USE:

- Cut out the ghosts and hang them from the ceiling with yarn or string to decorate the room for Halloween.
- Help the children tape their ghosts to paper sacks to make "spooky" trick or treat bags!

SUSPENDED SPIDER

MATERIALS:
- black tempera paint
- black and orange construction paper (8½" x 11")
- black yarn
- white chalk
- scissors
- glue
- ½" - 1" flat paintbrush
- newspaper

DIRECTIONS:
1. Spread newspaper over the work area.
2. Paint inside of palm and fingers, excluding thumb, with black paint.
3. With fingers slightly spread, press palm on orange construction paper so that fingers are pointing to the right side of the paper. Make an identical print with fingers pointing to the left side of the paper, overlapping the palm prints completely (see illustration).
4. Glue a piece of black yarn to the paper, extending from the top of the spider's body to the top of the page.
5. Cut a circle out of black construction paper (1½" - 2" in diameter), and glue it above the hand prints for the spider's head. Draw a face with white chalk.

USE:
- Make a large web using black yarn and attach it to the wall. Tape the children's spider prints to the web.

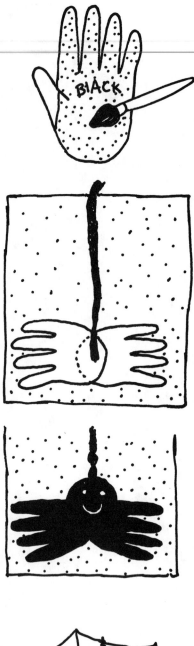

SCAREDY CAT

MATERIALS:
- black tempera paint
- orange and black construction paper (8½" x 11")
- pink and green construction paper scraps
- hole punch
- glue
- white chalk
- scissors
- ½" - 1" flat paintbrush
- newspaper

DIRECTIONS:
1. Spread newspaper over the work area.
2. Paint palm, thumb, and fingers of one hand with black paint.
3. With fingers spread and thumb at a right angle, press hand in the center of a sheet of orange construction paper.
4. While the hand print dries, cut a cat's head out of black construction paper using the pattern below.
5. Use a hole punch to punch holes out of green and pink construction paper. Glue two green eyes and a pink nose on the cat's head.
6. Glue the cat's head on the hand print body (the fingers become legs and the thumb becomes a tail).
7. Use white chalk to add features such as whiskers and a mouth.

HORN OF PLENTY

MATERIALS:
- tempera paint (brown, orange, yellow, purple, red, green, black)
- Manila paper (8½" x 11")
- ½" - 1" flat paintbrushes (one for each color)
- Styrofoam egg carton
- newspaper

DIRECTIONS:
1. Spread newspaper over the work area.
2. Pour a small amount of each color of paint into an egg carton cup.
3. Dip tip of index finger in brown paint and then paint a series of graduated, curved lines to form a cornucopia (see illustration).
4. Paint palm red, omitting thumb and fingers. Press palm near the top of the cornucopia opening to print an apple.
5. Dip pad of thumb in green paint. Print a leaf and stem on the apple. (Wipe off thumb.)
6. Dip pad of thumb in purple paint. Print a bunch of grapes underneath the apple.
7. Dip tip of index finger in yellow paint. Paint two curved lines to form a banana next to the apple.
8. Paint palm orange, omitting thumb and fingers. Press palm below the banana to print an orange.

USE:
- Ask each child to name one thing for which he or she is thankful. Write the words below the cornucopia prints and display the prints on a bulletin board for a Thanksgiving theme.

THANKSGIVING TURKEY

MATERIALS:
- tempera paint (brown, red, blue, green, yellow)
- crayons or felt-tip markers (black, orange, red)
- Manila paper (5" x 7")
- Sytrofoam egg carton
- ½" - 1" flat paintbrushes (one for each color)
- newspaper

DIRECTIONS:
1. Spread newspaper over the work area.
2. Pour a small amount of each color of paint in an egg carton cup.
3. Paint palm and inside of thumb brown.
4. Paint inside of each finger a different color. Paint one green, one red, one blue, and one yellow.
5. Spreading fingers and thumb as wide as possible, make a print near the center of the paper. (Press firmly to assure a good print.) Lift hand straight up to prevent smearing.
6. When the print is dry, use a crayon or marker to draw two black legs, each with three-pronged claws, extending from the bottom of the palm.
7. Draw an eye in the center of the thumb print with a black crayon or marker.
8. Draw an orange beak at the tip of the thumb print.
9. Draw a red wattle under the turkey's head.

INDIAN BRAVE

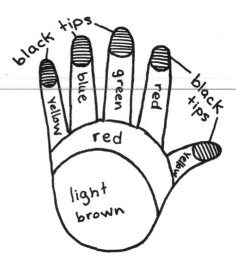

MATERIALS:

- tempera paint (light brown, black, red, blue, yellow, green, white)
- black felt-tip marker
- Manila paper (8½" x 11")
- Styrofoam egg carton
- ½" - 1" flat paintbrushes (one for each color)
- newspaper

DIRECTIONS:

1. Spread newspaper over the work area.
2. Pour a small amount of each color of paint into an egg carton cup.
3. Paint palm light brown, omitting thumb and fingers. (This will be the Indian's face.)
4. Paint tips of fingers and thumb black.
5. Using several colors, paint thumb and fingers to resemble feathers.
6. Paint a red headband beginning at the base of the thumb and extending around the base of the fingers.
7. Press hand firmly on the paper to make a print.
8. Wipe off index finger and dip it in brown paint. Print a nose on the side of the hand print opposite the thumb.
9. Dip another finger in black paint and print an eye on the Indian's face.
10. Draw a mouth under the Indian's nose with a black marker. Dab on war paint if desired.

22

SANTA CHRISTMAS CARD

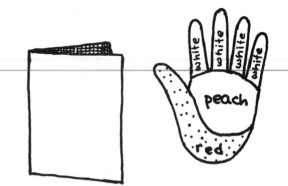

MATERIALS:
- tempera paint (red, peach, white, blue)
- Manila paper (8½" x 11")
- ½" - 1" flat paintbrushes (one for each color)
- newspaper

DIRECTIONS:
1. Spread newspaper over the work area.
2. Fold a sheet of Manila paper in half to make a card.
3. Paint lower palm and thumb red, middle palm peach, and fingers white (see illustration).
4. Make a print on the front of the card so that palm is pointing up and fingers are together and pointing down.
5. Dip tip of index finger in white paint and make a row of fingerprints between the peach and red sections to make the fur trim for Santa's hat. Make a white ball at the end of the thumb and two white circles in the peach section for Santa's cheeks.
6. Wipe off index finger and dip it in blue paint. Make two prints in the peach section for eyes.
7. Wipe off index finger and dip it in red paint. Print Santa's nose and mouth.

USE:
- Once the paint dries, have the children draw or write holiday messages inside their Santa cards. Let the children exchange cards with one another at a class party or take the cards home for someone special.

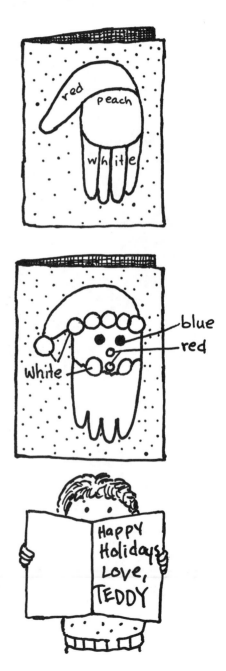

25

CHRISTMAS ANGEL

MATERIALS:

- tempera paint (white, peach, yellow, blue, pink)
- light blue construction paper (8½" x 11")
- gold sequins
- Styrofoam egg carton
- pan of soapy water and towel
- glue
- ½" - 1" flat paintbrushes (one for each color
- newspaper

DIRECTIONS:

1. Spread a thick layer of newspaper over the work area.
2. Place a pan of soapy water within easy reach.
3. Paint bottom of right foot white. Firmly press foot in the center of the paper. Rinse foot in soapy water and towel dry.
4. Paint inside of right hand white. Position hand over footprint, slightly overlapping the arch and angling toward the upper right-hand corner (see illustration). Press to make an angel's wing. Rinse and dry hand.
5. Paint palm peach, omitting thumb and fingers. Position palm at the heel of the footprint and press to form the angel's head (see illustration).
6. Dip tip of index finger in yellow paint (or other color) and "dot" hair on top of the angel's head.
7. Wipe off index finger and dip it in blue paint. Press finger tip on palm print to make eyes. Wipe off finger and dip it in pink paint. Make one pink dot under each eye for cheeks and a dot in the middle for a nose. Draw a mouth.

8. Glue gold sequins above the angel's head to make a halo.

USE:

- Help the children cut around their angel prints and glue the angels to white paper cups (with cups upside down). The children may take their angels home and place them atop their Christmas trees!

HOLIDAY WREATH

MATERIALS:

- red and green tempera paint
- red ribbon (1" - 2" wide, 24" long) or red paper bows
- white paper (20" square)
- ½" - 1" flat paintbrushes (one for each color)
- newspaper

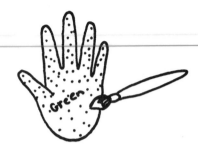

DIRECTIONS:

1. Spread newspaper over the work area.
2. Paint inside of hand, including fingers and thumb, with green paint. Print a circle of hands equidistant from the outer edge of the paper, reapplying paint as needed.
3. Dip pad of thumb in red paint and print red berries on the wreath.
4. Make a large bow using red ribbon and attach it to the wreath after the paint has dried (or attach red paper bows as desired).

USE:

- Display the wreaths around the classroom to add decoration for the holidays. Then, let the children take their wreaths home to hang on their own doors!

cheese!

29

O CHRISTMAS TREE

MATERIALS:

- tempera paint (green, red, yellow, blue)
- construction paper (12" x 18") or butcher paper
- ½" - 1" flat paintbrushes (one for each color)
- newspaper

DIRECTIONS:

1. Spread newspaper over the work area.
2. Paint inside of hand green, including fingers and thumb. Make hand prints to form a pyramid of the desired height. Begin at the top with one print and add one print to each row. Reapply paint as needed.
3. Make colorful thumb print ornaments to add the finishing touch.

USE:

- Have each child draw or paint beneath his or her tree pictures of gifts he or she would like to receive. Display the finished products on a bulletin board with the caption "Our Christmas Wishes."
- Let the class work together to make one large tree for the classroom door. Have each student make several hand prints until the tree is of the desired size. Children can make colorful palm prints, construction paper ornaments, paper chains, popcorn chains, and other decorations for the tree.

RUDOLPH

MATERIALS:
- tempera paint (brown, red, blue, tan)
- Manila paper or tagboard (8½" x 11")
- ½" - 1" flat paintbrushes (one for each color)
- pan of soapy water and towel
- newspaper

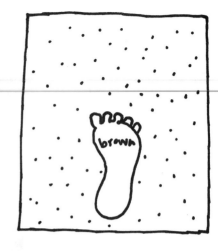

DIRECTIONS:
1. Spread newspaper over the work area.
2. Place a pan of soapy water within reach.
3. Paint bottom of foot brown. Make a print near the center bottom of the paper with toes pointing up. Wash and dry foot immediately.
4. Paint inside of each hand with tan paint, including thumbs and fingers. With fingers spread, make two prints at the edge of the toes to form antlers (see illustration).
5. Dip tip of index finger in blue paint and print two eyes.
6. Dip pad of thumb in red paint and print a nose near the center of the heel.

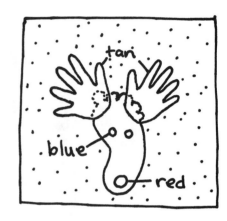

USE:
- Have the children make construction paper frames to glue around their Rudolph prints. Send the pictures home for special gifts.
- Tell the story of Rudolph before or after the activity. Recorded versions are also available and add flavor to story time.
- Substitute Rudolph prints for the bows on the holiday wreath (page 28).

HERE COMES SANTA CLAUS

MATERIALS:

- tempera paint (red, brown, peach, white)
- felt-tip markers (black, red, blue)
- white chalk
- dark blue construction paper (8½" x 14" or larger) or butcher paper
- ½" - 1" flat paintbrushes (one for each color)
- sponge
- pan of soapy water and towel
- newspaper

DIRECTIONS:

1. Spread newspaper over the work area. Place a pan of soapy water and a towel near the work area.
2. Paint bottom of right foot red, including toes. Press painted foot near the bottom right edge of the paper to make Santa's sleigh (see illustration). Immediately wash foot and towel dry.
3. Paint inside of left hand brown, including thumb and fingers. Press hand near heel with spread fingers pointing down and thumb at a right angle (see illustration). This print makes the reindeer.
4. Dip pad of thumb in peach paint and make a print near the big toe (see illustration).
5. When the paint dries, use markers to give Santa a red hat, blue eyes, a mouth and a nose. Use white chalk to draw Santa's beard and the fur trim on his hat.
6. Use a black marker to draw antlers, eyes, and reins on the reindeer.
7. Dip a sponge in white paint and squeeze it dry. Use the sponge to dab snow beneath the sleigh and reindeer.

USE:

- Let each child participate to make a mural. Have one child make the sleigh and have the other children make reindeer to pull the sleigh. Help the children add stars, rooftops, or whatever they choose to complete the mural. Hang the mural in the classroom or on the wall outside the classroom for everyone to enjoy.

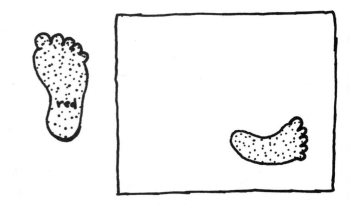

LACY VALENTINE

MATERIALS:
- red tempera paint
- white paper (8½" x 11")
- ½" - 1" flat paintbrush
- scissors
- paper doilies
- glue
- newspaper

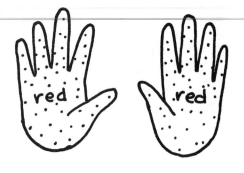

DIRECTIONS:
1. Spread newspaper over the work area.
2. Paint inside of both hands, including fingers and thumbs, with red paint.
3. Make two hand prints with hands at angles and fingers overlapping to form the point of the heart (see illustration). When the paint is dry, cut out the heart and glue it on a paper doily.

USE:
- Have the children glue their lacy valentines on large sheets of construction paper. Help the children write simple Valentine's Day messages on the papers with crayons or markers. Let the children exchange valentines or take them home for someone special.

if your doilies aren't big enough - use 3 small ones

GEORGE WASHINGTON'S CHERRY TREE

MATERIALS:
- tempera paint (red, green, brown)
- Manila paper (8½" x 11")
- ½" - 1" flat paintbrushes (one for each color)
- newspaper

DIRECTIONS:
1. Spread newspaper over the work area.
2. Paint inside of hand and fingers brown, excluding thumb. Make a print at the bottom center of a sheet of Manila paper (fingers pointing up).
3. Dip pad of thumb in green paint and make prints above and around the fingers for leaves.
4. Dip tip of index finger in red paint and print cherries on the tree.

You may want to partially paint the palm for a crooked tree trunk.

MARDI GRAS MASK

MATERIALS:
- tempera paint (colors of choice)
- 24" ribbon or yarn
- Manila tagboard (8½" x 11")
- Styrofoam egg carton
- ½" - 1" flat paintbrushes (one for each color)
- scissors
- glue

DIRECTIONS:
1. Spread newspaper over the work area.
2. Pour a small amount of each color of paint into an egg carton cup.
3. Paint inside of both hands, including fingers and thumbs. Use a stripe pattern, mixed colors, or other designs as you choose.
4. With fingers together and thumbs held close to palms, make two prints with heels of palms touching (fingers pointing up slightly — see illustration).
5. When the paint dries, cut around the mask being careful not to cut between the palms. Cut out eye holes in centers of palms.
6. Glue a ribbon to each side of the mask to tie the mask behind the head.

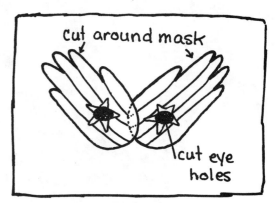

USE:
- Discuss the Mardi gras celebration. Have a Mardi gras party and let the children wear their masks!

41

SHAMROCKS FOR ST. PATRICK'S DAY

MATERIALS:

- green tempera paint
- Manila tagboard
- ½" - 1" flat paintbrush
- scissors
- yarn
- hole punch
- newspaper

DIRECTIONS:

1. Spread newspaper over the work area.
2. Paint inside of palm and fingers, omitting thumb, with green paint. Center the first print on the upper half of the paper with fingers pointing down. Make two additional hand prints, each at a right angle to the first, with palms pointing out and fingers overlapping slightly (see illustration).
3. Use three fingers to paint a stem under the clover leaves.

USE:

- Help the children cut out their shamrocks, punch holes in the tops, and thread yarn through the holes. The children will enjoy wearing their shamrock necklaces on St. Patrick's Day!

43

LIVELY LEPRECHAUN

MATERIALS:

- tempera paint (green, peach, white, black, pink)
- construction paper (8½" x 11")
- red felt-tip marker
- ½" - 1" flat paintbrushes (one for each color)
- newspaper

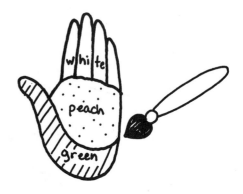

DIRECTIONS:

1. Spread newspaper over the work area.
2. Paint lower palm and thumb green and middle palm peach (see illustration).
3. Paint inside of fingers white.
4. Make a print with thumb slightly extended and fingers pointing down.
5. Dip tip of index finger in blue paint and make two eyes in the peach section.
6. Dip pad of thumb in pink paint and print two cheeks and a nose.
7. When the paint has dried, draw a happy smile with a red marker.

USE:

- Make a lively display for the classroom or hall. Paint or draw a large rainbow and a pot of gold on white butcher paper. Cut out the drawing and attach it to the wall. Display the completed leprechauns on and around the rainbow.

44

WAVING WINDMILL

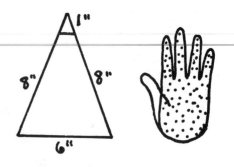

MATERIALS:

- tempera paint (color of choice)
- construction paper of any color (8½" x 11")
- light blue construction paper (8½" x 11")
- ½" - 1" flat paintbrush
- glue
- scissors
- newspaper

DIRECTIONS:

1. Spread newspaper over the work area.
2. Cut a triangle with a six-inch base and eight-inch sides out of construction paper of any color. Cut off the top point of the triangle about one inch from the top.
3. Glue the triangle near the bottom edge of a sheet of blue construction paper.
4. Paint inside of hand and fingers, excluding thumb, any color.
5. Make four prints at the top of the windmill base for blades. Be sure that fingers are together and palms are touching (see illustration).

USE:

- Create an attractive springtime presentation by displaying the windmills with the tulip prints (page 48).

46

TULIP PARADE

MATERIALS:

- tempera paint (blue, red, yellow, green)
- Manila paper or construction paper (8½" x 11")
- ½" - 1" flat paintbrushes (one for each color)
- newspaper

DIRECTIONS:

1. Spread newspaper over the work area.
2. Paint palm and fingers, excluding thumb, with paint of the desired color.
3. Make a print, fingers together and pointing up, near the top of the paper.
4. Dip tip of index finger in green paint and paint a stem from the bottom edge of the hand print to the bottom of the page. Then paint two leaves.

USE:

- Display the tulips on a bulletin board with the caption "Tulips on Parade."
- Line up the completed tulip prints to make an attractive border for a bulletin board, wall, door, or window display.

COLORFUL EGG BASKET

MATERIALS:
- tempera paint (pastel colors)
- Manila paper or pastel construction paper (8½" x 11")
- ½" - 1" flat paintbrushes (one for each color)
- Styrofoam egg carton
- newspaper

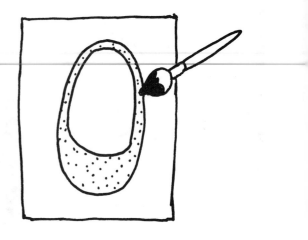

DIRECTIONS:
1. Spread newspaper over the work area.
2. Pour a small amount of each color of paint into an egg carton cup.
3. Paint a simple basket on a sheet of paper or trace the pattern on page 51.
4. Dip pad of thumb in paint and randomly print a basketful of colorful eggs.

USE:
- To make a colorful display, group the basket prints with the bunny prints (page 52) on a bulletin board or wall. Make grass by fringing a long strip of green construction paper and curling the paper around a pencil.

SPRINGTIME BUNNY

MATERIALS:
- white and pink tempera paint
- pastel construction paper (8½" x 11")
- ½" - 1" flat paintbrushes (one for each color)
- white chalk
- black crayon
- newspaper

DIRECTIONS:
1. Spread newspaper over the work area.
2. Paint palm and fingers white, omitting thumb. Press hand on paper, being sure to leave space between the two middle fingers so that each pair of fingers forms an ear.
3. Dip pad of thumb in pink paint and print eyes and a nose.
4. Use a black crayon to draw a mouth, whiskers, and two front teeth. Color the teeth with white chalk.

use pink paint or chalk to fill in the insides of ears

53

MOTHER'S DAY HUG

MATERIALS:

- tempera paint (any color)
- white butcher paper
- scissors
- glue
- crayons or pencils
- ribbon
- newspaper

DIRECTIONS:

1. Spread newspaper over the work area.
2. Cut a strip of white paper as long as the child's arm span. Trim the paper so that it is approximately six inches wide.
3. Paint insides of both hands, including thumbs. Make a hand print at each end of the paper (fingers pointing "out").
4. When the prints are dry, cut around each hand to give definition (leaving the strip intact).
5. Attach a copy of the "Hug-A-Bunch" poem to the center of the strip (see page 55).
6. Write "Happy Mother's Day" to the left of the poem and "Love (child's name)" to the right of the poem. (Have each child write this. Assist as necessary.) Add a date if desired.
7. Roll the paper into a scroll and tie it with ribbon.

USE:

- Let the children take their "Mother's Day Hugs" home for extra special Mother's Day gifts!

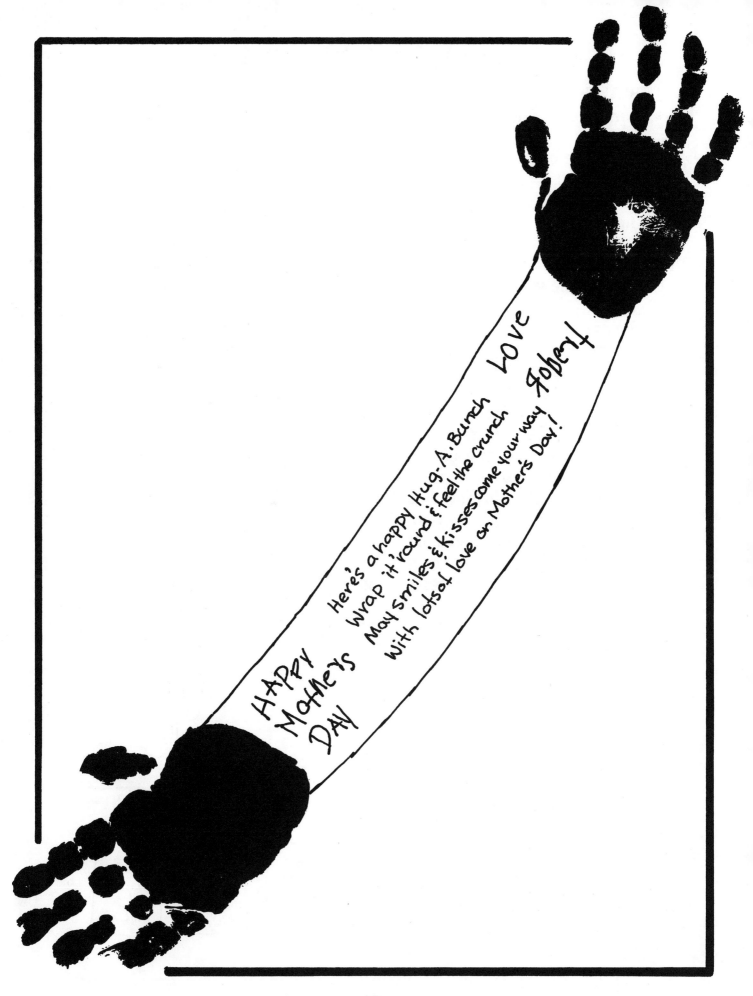

Here's a happy Hug-A-Bunch
Wrap it 'round & feel the crunch
May smiles & kisses come your way
With lots of love on Mother's Day!

Love
Robert

HAPPY
Mother's
DAY

SASSY SUNFLOWER

MATERIALS:

- tempera paint (yellow, brown, green)
- light blue butcher paper
- ½" - 1" flat paintbrushes (one for each color)
- newspaper

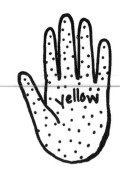

DIRECTIONS:

1. Spread newspaper over the work area.
2. Paint inside of hand, including fingers and thumb, with yellow paint. With fingers slightly spread, make eight hand prints to form a circle. Be sure that each print touches another print and that fingers are pointing away from the center of the circle. Reapply paint as necessary.

3. Dip pad of thumb in brown paint and fill the center of the circle with prints.
4. Dip two fingers in green paint. With fingers together, paint a stem from the bottom of the flower to the bottom of the paper.
5. Paint inside of palm or index finger green and print leaves on the stem as desired.

USE:

- Group the completed sunflower prints on a wall or bulletin board to make a beautiful spring flower garden!

BOUNCING BUTTERFLY

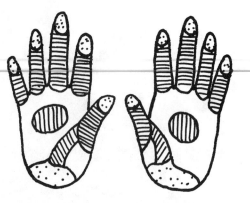

MATERIALS:
- tempera paint (colors of your choice)
- construction paper (8½" x 11")
- scissors
- ½" - 1" flat paintbrushes (one for each color)
- Styrofoam egg carton
- newspaper

DIRECTIONS:
1. Spread newspaper over the work area.
2. Pour a small amount of each color of tempera paint in an egg carton cup.
3. Paint inside of each hand using any colors and patterns. Try to make each hand a mirror image of the other.
4. With fingers slightly spread, make a print with each hand so that palms touch and thumbs overlap (see illustration). Then, turn the paper upside down and make two more prints so that the heels of the palms overlap those of the first prints (see illustration).
5. Dip finger tip in paint and print two "feelers," one extending from each thumb at the "top" of the butterfly. Add a finger tip print at the end of each feeler.

58

CLASSY CATERPILLAR

MATERIALS:
- tempera paint (color of your choice)
- ½" - 1" flat paintbrush
- butcher paper
- black marker or crayon
- newspaper

DIRECTIONS:
1. Spread newspaper over the work area.
2. Paint teacher's palm, omitting fingers and thumb, and make a print in the middle of one end of the paper. (This makes the caterpillar's head.)
3. Paint the palm and fingers, omitting thumb, of each child. Have each child make a print to form the caterpillar's "body." Fingers should point down and prints should touch but not overlap.
4. Draw eyes, a happy smile, and a pair of "feelers" on the caterpillar's head with a black crayon or marker.

USE:
- Use the completed caterpillar as a border for a bulletin board or display.
- After the paint dries, have each child write his or her name on a hand print. Display the "classy caterpillar" on the wall outside the classroom.

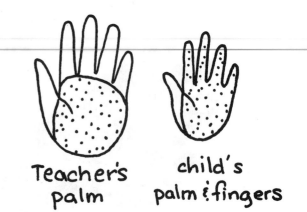

Teacher's palm   child's palm & fingers

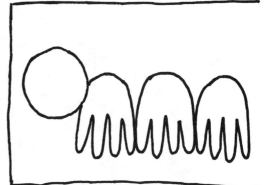

make a curvy caterpillar if you like

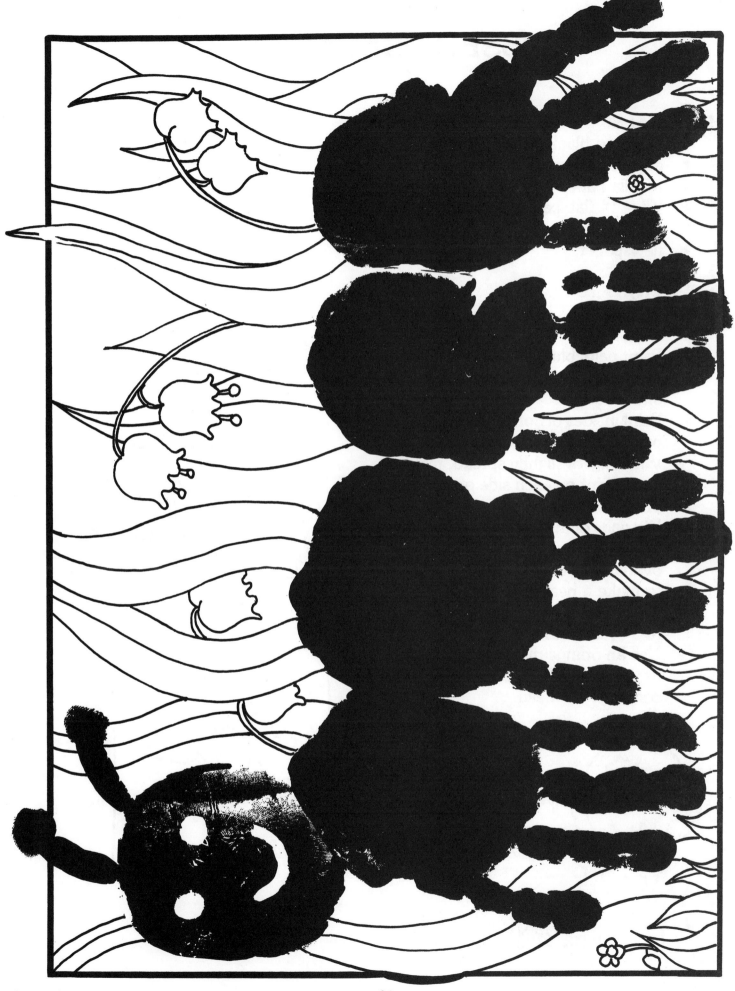

61

BLISSFUL BLUEBIRD

MATERIALS:
- blue and black tempera paint
- orange crayon or marker
- Manila paper (8½" x 11")
- ½" - 1" flat paintbrushes (one for each color)
- newspaper

DIRECTIONS:
1. Spread newspaper over the work area.
2. Paint palm blue. Make a print in the center of a sheet of paper to form the bird's body.
3. Paint insides of both hands with blue paint, including fingers and thumbs. With fingers slightly spread, make a hand print on each side of the palm print to form wings (see illustration).
4. Dip pads of thumbs in blue paint and make two thumb prints side by side, overlapping the top of the palm print to make a head (see illustration).
5. Dip finger in black paint and print two eyes on the head.
6. Use an orange marker or crayon to draw a triangular beak at the bottom center of the head.

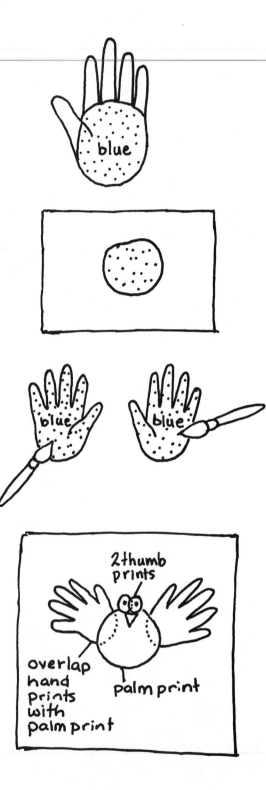

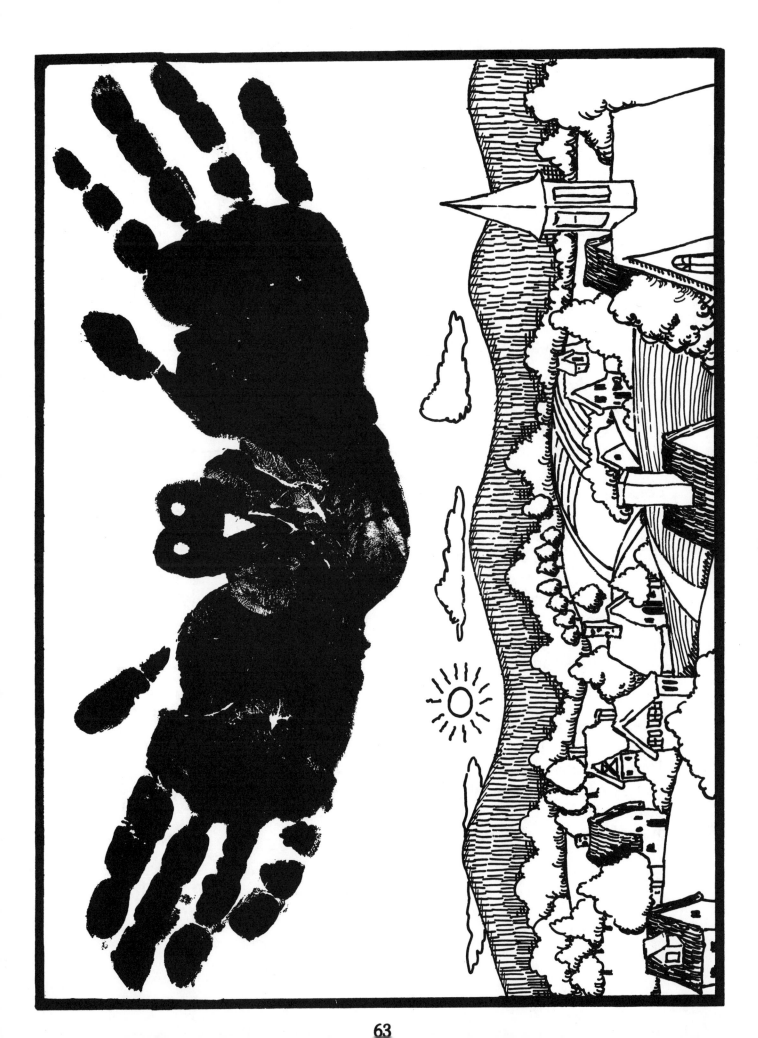

SPLENDID SWAN

MATERIALS:
- white and blue tempera paint
- blue construction paper (8½" x 11")
- ½" - 1" flat paintbrush
- orange and black felt-tip markers
- small sponge
- newspaper

DIRECTIONS:
1. Spread newspaper over the work area.
2. Paint inside of palm, fingers, and thumb with white paint.
3. With fingers together and thumb at a right angle, make a print in the center of a sheet of blue construction paper (thumb pointing up).
4. Make a small dot in the center of the thumb print with a black marker.
5. Use an orange marker to draw a beak near the top of the thumb print.
6. Dip a sponge in blue paint and squeeze it dry. Dab blue water around the swan.

USE:
- Present this as a follow-up activity after reading "The Ugly Duckling." Help each child write one thing that makes him or her special below the swan print. Display the pictures on a bulletin board with the caption "(teacher's name)'s Splendid Swans."

ELROY ELEPHANT

MATERIALS:
- light and dark gray tempera paint
- black felt-tip marker
- white chalk
- ½" - 1" flat paintbrushes (one for each color)
- construction paper of any color (8½" x 11")
- newspaper

DIRECTIONS:
1. Spread newspaper over the work area.
2. Paint inside of hand, including fingers and thumb, with light gray paint.
3. With fingers and thumb spread wide, center hand on construction paper and make a print (fingers pointing down).
4. Dip pad of thumb in dark gray paint and print an ear on the ball of the palm print (see illustration).
5. Draw an eye and a tail with a black marker.
6. Draw a tusk with white chalk.

66

LEO LION

MATERIALS:
- tempera paint (gold, black, green)
- black felt-tip marker
- Manila paper (8½" x 11")
- scissors
- glue
- newspaper

DIRECTIONS:
1. Spread newspaper over the work area.
2. Paint inside of hand, including fingers and thumb, with gold paint.
3. With fingers and thumb spread wide, make a print in the center of a sheet of Manila paper (fingers pointing down, thumb at right angle).
4. Cut a circle out of gold construction paper for the lion's head. Make short cuts all around the circle to make a mane (see illustration). Curl the mane around a finger or pencil to give it shape. Glue the lion's head on the print so that it overlaps the heel of the palm (side opposite thumb).
5. Dip finger in green paint and print two eyes. (Wipe off finger.)
6. Dip finger in black paint and print a nose.
7. Draw a lion's mouth and whiskers with a black marker.

LITTLE PONY

MATERIALS:

- tempera paint (colors of choice)
- felt-tip markers (black and other colors of choice)
- construction paper of any color (8½" x 11")
- ½" - 1" flat paintbrushes (one for each color)
- newspaper

DIRECTIONS:

1. Spread newspaper over the work area.
2. Paint inside of hand, including thumb and fingers, with any color of tempera paint.
3. With fingers spread and thumb extended at a right angle, make a print in the center of a sheet of construction paper (fingers pointing down).
4. Use a black marker to draw a mouth, nose, and eye on the thumb print. Add two pointed ears.
5. Dip finger in contrasting color of paint and paint a mane and tail. Use the tip of a finger to "dot" a hoof at the end of each fingerprint. Add fingerprint spots, if desired.

70

OLLIE OCTOPUS

MATERIALS:

- tempera paint (black and other colors as desired)
- Manila paper (8½" x 11")
- blue construction paper (8½" x 11")
- ½" - 1" flat paintbrushes (one for each color)
- glue
- scissors
- newspaper

DIRECTIONS:

1. Spread newspaper over the work area.
2. Paint inside of hand, excluding thumb, any color. Press painted hand onto paper with spread fingers pointing down. (Two or three colors make an attractive octopus.)
3. Make a second print, overlapping the first in the palm area and positioning the fingers between the first fingerprints, so that a body and eight legs are formed (see illustration). Reapply paint before the second printing, if necessary.
4. Dip finger tip in black paint and print two eyes and a mouth.
5. When the octopus is dry, cut it out and glue it on a blue paper ocean.

RAINBOW FISH

MATERIALS:

- tempera paint (rainbow colors)
- Manila paper (8½" x 11")
- blue construction paper (8½" x 11")
- ½" – 1" flat paintbrushes (one for each color)
- glue
- scissors
- newspaper

DIRECTIONS:

1. Spread newspaper over the work area.
2. Paint palm and fingers, excluding thumb, with a rainbow of colors (see illustration).
3. With fingers together, make a print on Manila paper.
4. Dip tip of index finger in any color of paint. Make two fingerprints side by side at the end of the palm print for a mouth. Make another fingerprint on the palm for an eye.
5. Dip index finger in the color of your choice and paint fins and a tail (see illustration).
6. When the fish is dry, cut it out and glue it on a blue paper ocean.

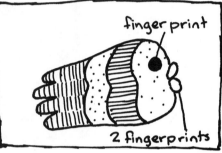

USE:

- Create an ocean scene bulletin board complete with seaweed, rocks, and a sunken treasure chest. Cut out the fish and attach them to the board.

FLORIDA BLUE CRAB

MATERIALS:

- blue and orange tempera paint
- construction paper (8½" x 11")
- ½" - 1" flat paintbrush
- black felt-tip marker
- newspaper

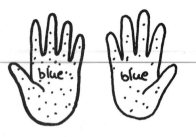

DIRECTIONS:

1. Spread newspaper over the work area.
2. Paint inside of both hands, including thumbs and fingers, with blue paint.
3. Make two prints with hands pointing in opposite directions and heels of palms slightly overlapping (thumbs pointing down — see illustration).

4. Dip tip of finger in orange paint and draw two "stalks" (for eyes) extending from the palm area (see illustration). Print a dot at the end of each stalk and add an eye inside each dot with a black marker.
5. Dip pad of thumb in orange paint and make a print at the end of each thumb print for claws. Draw a smile with a black marker.

USE:

- Create a seashore bulletin board scene on which to display the children's crabs.

PATRIOTIC BANNER

MATERIALS:
- tempera paint (red, white, blue)
- white or silver star
- Manila paper (8½" x 11")
- ½" - 1" flat paintbrushes (one for each color)
- newspaper

DIRECTIONS:
1. Spread newspaper over the work area.
2. Paint inside of hand to resemble a flag (see illustration). Paint thumb white. Paint a blue square in the corner next to the white thumb. Alternate red and white paint on each finger, extending the paint into the palm to form stripes.
3. Make a print with fingers together and thumb at a right angle (thumb pointing down).
4. When the paint is dry, glue a star in the center of the blue square.

USE:
- Back each print with sturdy construction paper or poster board. Cut out the banners and glue them to craft sticks or tongue depressors.
- Cover a bulletin board with the completed banners to make a patriotic display. Trim the board in red, white, and blue!